24 Day Challenge Cookbook

By;

Chef James Shipley and Pam S. Heintz

A note from the Chef:

You will notice throughout this cookbook that I reference the use of a particular brand of product to use in conjunction with this cookbook. I do so because I believe that this product is of the highest quality and has the best nutritional value. I do not represent the company and receive no remuneration for this endorsement.

Table of contents

Shopping List................................Pg 3

24 day Challenge Meal Guide   Pg 5

Food prep tips   Pg 7

First 10 days food schedule and recipes   Pg 14

Day 11- 24 food schedule and recipes   Pg 16

Snacks and Appetizers   Pg 20

Salads and Dressings   Pg 25

Soups   Pg 39

Wraps and Sandwiches   Pg 49

Entrees   Pg 55

Desserts   Pg 77

Odds and Ends   Pg 81

Index   Pg 86

24 Day Challenge
Shopping list Guidelines

FOODS AND INGREDIENTS TO AVOID:

>Sugar, Mayonnaise, Cereal, Fruit Juice (eat fruit instead) Processed Foods, Canned Vegetables (except tomatoes) Canned Fruit, White Sauces, Cheese Sauces, Alcohol, Bacon, Sausage, Hydrogenated oils, High fructose corn syrup, Margarine, Coffee, soda pop, wheat flour (use whole grain flours), High Fat Dairy

PRODUCE: Fresh produce when possible, Frozen is better than canned

Dark Leaf Lettuces	Avocado
Tomatoes	Onions
Carrots	Green Peppers
Celery	Cucumbers
Sprouts	Spinach
Radishes	Broccoli
Cabage	Dried Beans
Asparagus	Green Beans
Leeks	Okra
Peas	Turnips
Egg Plant	Spaghetti Squash
Butternut Squash,	Acorn Squash
Sweet Potatoes	Zucchini
Brussel sprouts	
Apples	Bananas
Cherries	Blueberries
Grape fruit	Grapes
Melons	Kiwi Fruit

Peaches	Pears
Plums	Raisins
Nectarine	Mango
Oranges	Strawberries
Lemons / Limes	Pineapple

Lean meats and proteins

Skinless Chicken Breast
Salmon (also in burgers)
Tilapia
Pork Chops
Whole & Ground Turkey (also in burgers)
Veggie Burgers
Tuna (fresh or canned in water)
Any White Fish
Eggs
Lean Beef
Ham (in moderation)
Bison
Duck

BREAD:

Multi Grain and Whole grain (no fructose)

SNACKS:

Natural Peanut Butter
Rice Cakes
All Kinds of Nuts and Seeds
ApplesauceCups (no fructose corn syrup)
Fruit Cups   (no syrup)
Advocare Snack and Meal Replacement Bars
Low fat Yogurt (after day 10)

Remember, THIS IS NOT A DIET!!!
This is a challenge to change your thinking and
behavior as it relates to consuming food.

Use this chart to make better food choices. You will be
amazed how quickly eating well and cooking well will make
you feel well.

* = recipes in the cookbook.

*DAYS 1 – 10 AVOID: Fried Foods, Processed Foods,
All Dairy, Sugar, Soda Pop, Alcohol, Coffee*

*DAYS 1 – 10 ALLOWED: Unlimited Fruits & vegetables,
Oatmeal, Hummus, Nuts, Eggs, Olive Oil, Lean Meats
(Chicken, Salmon, etc.) Brown Rice, Avocado, Natural
Peanut Butter (peanuts only ingredient) Sweet Potatoes,
Multi Grain Bread (no Fructose Corn Syrup)*

*DAYS 11 – 24 ALLOWED FOODS: Same as days 1 – 10, one
glass of wine per day, Low fat/ No fat dairy, lean lunch
meats*

Breakfast: Every morning have an Advocare Meal
Replacement Shake and a Spark energy drink. Here are
some ideas.
You will need a blender. Try 2-3 ice cubes, or add; 1 – 2
tablespoons of natural peanut butter and/ or a banana.
or; 1/3 cup frozen berries or other frozen fruit. Also try
adding one pouch or scoop of Spark. Mandarin Orange in
Choc. Yumm!

A.M. & P.M. SNACKS: Drink a Spark 30 mins. before or with snack. *Days 1–10 Try to avoid dairy.* . Also try to keep all snacks under 300 calories for best results

Fresh fruit & vegetables are best for an unlimited snack

Here are some ideas for other snacks. *Hummus on celery or carrot sticks. Oatmeal plain or sugar free, 2 slices of Multi-Grain bread or toast with natural peanut butter . *2 Hard boiled or pickled eggs, Rice cakes, Multi-Grain crackers, Nuts and *Nut mixes. * Cinnamon Almond Raisin Low fat yogurt Clusters

. LUNCH: *Days 11-24 don't forget to take your MNS pack 30 mins. before lunch.*

Salads make a great lunch meal. You can eat as big a salad of greens as you can eat. Use our salad topper ideas to balance out your meal and satisfy you till your P.M. snack.

Tuna with olives, capers or artichokes,   *Southwest Chicken Salad,   *Ham & Egg Salad, Bean or Alfalfa Sprouts,

Sliced bell peppers or avocoda, *Salsa,   *Artisans Chicken Salad,   *Cole Slaw,   *Mediterranean Salad

Other lunch ideas:

Japanese Cucumber Salad with Egg Drop Soup, * Chili, *Hummus Veggie Sandwich, Veggie Omelet, *Chicken Rice Soup, *Black Bean Soup,   *Tomato Basil Soup, Turkey Burger,   Tuna Salad Lettuce Wrap,

* Blue Pear Pizza (amazing!!!)   *Pizza on whole wheat crust,

DINNER: *Use any of the lunch ideas for dinner as well.*

Serve with fresh green salad, *steamed vegetables and multi-grain bread for a balanced satisfying meal.

*Stuffed Green Peppers, * Lemon Caper Chicken over Brn. Rice, *3 Sisters, *Grilled Tilapia, Baked Sweet Potatoes,
Veggie Frittata, *Pork Chop w/ sauerkraut & squash, Salmon Burgers, Crockpot roast,
*Vegetable Curry on Brn. Rice
*Ratatouille, *Asian Noodles w/ peanut sauce, * Mujadara and Cucumber Salad, *Broccoli Ginger Stir-fry
*Spaghetti Squash with Marinara sauce, Shish-Kabobs, Grilled
Portobello
Mushroom

24 Day CHALLENGE Food Prep Tips

1. COOK IN BULK. If you are going to take the time to cook, make large batches and store or freeze things. Freeze single serving sizes in microwave safe containers. This gives the convenience of store bought frozen dinners but without the cost and all the chemical preservatives.

2. COUNT TIME VERSES COST. During this challenge you will eating a lot of fresh fruits and vegetables. There are many pre-cut foods in the produce departments. You will have to decide if you to take the time to cut, slice and prep fruits and veggies which will save money, or buy the pre packaged items

to save time. If you buy pre packaged produce, READ THE LABLES. Avoid preservatives and chemical additives.

3. WHAT TYPE OF FOOD TO BUY? **Grocery store** fresh produce is *good*. Frozen vegetables are better than canned *with the exception of canned tomatoes.* **Organic** produce is *better* because it is grown without chemical pesticides and fertilizers. **HOME GROWN** produce is the *best!!!* Make a plan to grow some of your own food. Even if you don't have garden space, you can use large clay pots or even 5 gallon plastic buckets and put them on a sunny porch. Nothing tastes better than fresh vegetables right off the vine.

4. CONVIENCENCE FOODS. There is no harm in buying prepared whole foods as a time saver. Better to run into the grocery and buy a bag of pre made salad, a loaf of fresh multi grain bread or rolls and a roasted whole chicken than to run through a fast food drive thru. The walk through the aisles is more exercise than sitting in your car at the drive-thru window!!! Just be sure you READ THE LABLES. If there are ingredients that don't grow in a garden or come from a cow, pig, chicken or fish, think twice about buying it.

5. PREPING CHICKEN AND BEEF. Boneless-skinless chicken breasts are very convenient to use. After you bake them in the oven, slice them diagonally and package individual servings in microwave/ freezer safe containers or zip-lock bags. They are now available to use on salads and other dishes. Just put

them in the microwave oven for 45 seconds. Heat longer on a lower temperature setting if not hot enough. Beef roast can be packaged & frozen the same way.

Whole chickens can be baked in the oven or a crockpot. When chicken is done, remove all the skin, de-bone the meat, package and freeze. You can use the bones (minus the skin) to make chicken broth by adding 8-10 cups of water in a large pot. Add 1 small diced onion, 1-2 stalks of diced celery and 1 chopped carrot. Cook on stovetop on low or in a crockpot for 2-3 hours.

6.   SPICES AND SEASONINGS. Spice, herbs, and seasonings are low in calories and big on flavor! Be creative, experiment with different spices. (Hint: try to write down what and how much of different spices & herbs you use. That way if it's really good you can repeat it.) **McKay's Instant Broth and Seasonings** are VERY GOOD products. They offer gluten free, vegan, no MSG product that taste amazing!!! Find McKay's on e-bay or in most health food stores.

The next six pages is a chart you may use for making your food choices for each day. This chart is merely a guide and does not have to strictly adhered to.

You are welcome to choose any foods and recipes in this book. During your first ten days of the Challenge, avoid those dishes with dairy. These food choices and recipes are designed to give you the maximum benefit during this phase.

Important note: It is critical to eat every few hours! Don't go more than three hours without a snack. You will boost your metabolism and reduce the desire to binge eat. It doesn't have to be much, but if you get really hungry, there is no reason not to have another breakfast shake or a meal replacement bar.

Breakfast:

During the 24 day challenge you start each day with a delicious shake below are some ideas to create even more variety with your options. If you find that after having a spark and a breakfast shake, you are still hungry, then snack! Fresh fruit or veggies is best. Try and avoid cereals. They have lots of good nutrition, but are not well balanced with protein. The carbohydrates to protein ratio that we start the day with is crucial. This program starts you with an even 1 to 1 ratio. What does that mean? It means good sustained energy and reduced hunger.

B

Ideas for shakes:

Berry:

Classic: ice and water

Banana, mixed fruit, mango and pineapple, lowfat yogurt, blueberry, strawberries, cherries, etc...

Try frozen fruit and skip the ice.

Vanilla: same as berry, but with even more options

I love the vanilla with mango and pineapple. How frozen cherries? Banana and strawberry. Try bananas, natural peanut butter and maybe a scoop of cocoa powder. Play around, the combinations are limitless!

Chocolate: By now you should get the idea. How about Cherries and chocolate? PB and chocolate, banana chocolate, or add TBSP cocoa powder to have chocolate madness!

Eating out.

There are lots of great recipes that you can make in bulk and bring with you each day. But we all know that won't happen every time. Eventually you will end up having to eat out. It is not hard to make good choices. Many restaurants have menus that list healthy choices, take advantage of these options. Don't be afraid to ask your server to modify a meal. Instead of mashed potatoes and gravy, perhaps a sweet potato? Instead of french fries, how about some steamed broccoli? It's no trouble, servers understand.

Accept challenges, so that you may feel the exhilaration of victory.
  -George S. Patton

Snacks for days 1 - 10

Fresh Fruit   Mellon, Banana, Bing Cherries,
 Carrot & Celery Sticks w/ Hummus
seedless grapes and a handful of nuts
Rice cakes

Snacks for days 11 - 24

PB & Banana Sandwich,   Trail mix, Oat Meal,
 Carrot & Celery Sticks w/ Hummus
Salsa on Whole wheat pita bread
Cinnamon Almond Raisin Clusters .
Rice cakes

Happiness comes of the capacity to feel deeply,
to enjoy simply, to think freely, to risk life, to be
needed

  - Storm Jameson

Day 1	Day 2
Breakfast	**Breakfast**
Advocare Meal Replacement Shake Fiber Drink (mix separately)	Advocare Meal Replacement Shake Fiber Drink (mix separately)
Morning Snack	**Morning Snack**
Lunch	**Lunch**
Fresh Salsa on Chicken Salad Pg. 26	Chicken Red Bell Pepper Salad Pg. 29
Afternoon Snack	**Afternoon Snack**
Dinner	**Dinner**
Pan Seared Tilapia Pg. 56 White bean puree Pg. 82	Lemon Caper Chicken Over Brown Rice pg. 63 Side Salad
Day 3	Day 4
Breakfast	**Breakfast**
Advocare Meal Replacement Shake Fiber Drink (mix separately)	Advocare Meal Replacement Shake In a Blender, try adding 1/3 c Fresh or frozen Blueberries
Morning Snack	**Morning Snack**
Lunch	**Lunch**
Turkey Burger on Multi-grain bun With lettuce, tomato, sliced onion	Large mixed greens salad With sliced green bell peppers avocado
Afternoon Snack	**Afternoon Snack**
Dinner	**Dinner**
Stuffed Green Peppers Pg. 61 Side Salad	Ginger Chicken Cups Pg. 51 Steamed Snow Peas Multi grain roll

Day 5	Day 6
Breakfast	**Breakfast**
Advocare Meal Replacement Shake	Advocare Meal Replacement Shake
Morning Snack	**Morning Snack**
Lunch	**Lunch**
Tuna and Green Olives Over salad greens With Shinny Dressing pg.36	Hummus Veggie Wrap Pg. 50
Afternoon Snack	**Afternoon Snack**
Dinner	**Dinner**
Ratatouille Pg. 62 Side Salad Multi grain roll	Southwest Chicken Salad Pg. 31 Steamed Green Beans
Day 7	**Day 8**
Breakfast	**Breakfast**
Advocare Meal Replacement Shake	Advocare Meal Replacement Shake Fiber Drink (mix separately)
Morning Snack	**Morning Snack**
Lunch	**Lunch**
Chili Pg. 40	Chicken Vegetable Soup Pg. 46 Large mixed greens salad
Afternoon Snack	**Afternoon Snack**
Dinner	**Dinner**
Mujadarar Pg. 64 Salad with cucumber dressing Pg. 36	Pork Chops w/ sauerkraut & squash pg. 69 Side Salad

Day 9	Day 10
Breakfast	**Breakfast**
Advocare Meal Replacement Shake Fiber Drink (mix separately)	Advocare Meal Replacement Shake Fiber Drink (mix separately)
Morning Snack	**Morning Snack**
Lunch	**Lunch**
Mediterranean Salad Pg. 28 Whole wheat pita bread And Hummus	Beet Salad Pg. 38
Afternoon Snack	**Afternoon Snack**
Dinner	**Dinner**
Vegetable Curry on Brown Rice Pg. 75 Side Salad	Cod with Tomato Relish Pg. 57 Side Salad
Day 11	**Day 12**
Breakfast	**Breakfast**
Advocare Meal Replacement Shake	Advocare Meal Replacement Shake
Morning Snack	**Morning Snack**
Lunch	**Lunch**
Blue Pear Pizza Pg. 66 Side Salad	Root Vegetable Stew Pg. 42
Afternoon Snack	**Afternoon Snack**
Dinner	**Dinner**
Spaghetti Squash With Marinara Pg. 72 Side Salad Multi grain garlic bread	Grilled Cocoa Chicken Pg. 66 Steamed Asparagus

Day 13	Day 14
Breakfast	**Breakfast**
Advocare Meal Replacement Shake	Advocare Meal Replacement Shake
Morning Snack	Morning Snack
Lunch	**Lunch**
Black Bean Soup pg. 48 Salsa on mixed greens	Quinoa Salad Pg. 43
Afternoon Snack	Afternoon Snack
Dinner	**Dinner**
Salmon Burgers	Blue Pear Pizza Pg. 66
Day 15	Day 16
Breakfast	**Breakfast**
Advocare Meal Replacement Shake	Advocare Meal Replacement Shake
Morning Snack	Morning Snack
Lunch	**Lunch**
Mushroom Philly Sub On multi grain bun Pg. 54	Mushroom Barley Soup Pg. 41
Afternoon Snack	Afternoon Snack
Dinner	**Dinner**
Veggie Bake Pg. 67	Sauteed chick w/ kale and mushrooms Pg. 69

Day 17	Day 18
Breakfast	**Breakfast**
Advocare Meal Replacement Shake	Advocare Meal Replacement Shake
Morning Snack	**Morning Snack**
Lunch	**Lunch**
Curried Chicken Salad Pg. 32	Artisans Chicken Salad Pg. 30
Afternoon Snack	**Afternoon Snack**
Dinner	**Dinner**
Butternut Squash Pasta Pg. 71 Green beans	Sweet Potato, Corn and Black Bean fry up Pg. 65 Side Salad
Day 19	Day 20
Breakfast	**Breakfast**
Advocare Meal Replacement Shake	Advocare Meal Replacement Shake
Morning Snack	**Morning Snack**
Lunch	**Lunch**
Quick Mesclun Salad Pg. 34 Tomato Basil Soup Pg. 44	Lentil Soup Pg.45 Whole wheat pita wedges
Afternoon Snack	**Afternoon Snack**
Dinner	**Dinner**
Pork Tenderloin with Apples Salad Pg. 68	Three bean Tacos Pg.73

Day 21	Day 22
Breakfast	**Breakfast**
Advocare Meal Replacement Shake	Advocare Meal Replacement Shake
Morning Snack	Morning Snack
Lunch	**Lunch**
Veggie Anitpasto Pg. 37	Chicken, bell pepper salad Pg. 29
Afternoon Snack	Afternoon Snack
Dinner	**Dinner**
Baked Orange Chicken with Broccoli Pg. 70	Asian Noodle Salad with peanut sauce Pg. 76
Day 23	Day 24
Breakfast	**Breakfast**
Advocare Meal Replacement Shake	Advocare Meal Replacement Shake
Morning Snack	Morning Snack
Lunch	**Lunch**
Veggie Sandwich Pg. 53	Jamaican Rundown Soup Pg. 43
Afternoon Snack	Afternoon Snack
Dinner	**Dinner**
Veggie Bake Pg. 67	3 Sisters Pg. 60

Snacks

and

Appetizers

Good news!! On the 24 day challenge, not only are you allowed to snack, you are encouraged to snack!!

There are a few guidelines for snacking to improve your success of weight loss while on the challenge. Days 1 – 10, fresh fruit and raw vegetables are the best for snacking.

Traditional Hummus

In a food processor put;
2 cups   cooked or canned Chick Peas (drained)
2 Tbsp   Lemon Juice
¼ cup   Tahini
1 tsp   minced Garlic or 1 clove minced
1 tsp   Salt
1 cup   extra Virgin Olive Oil

Blend together

Add ¼ - 1/3 cup of Water till hummus is smooth and creamy

Roasted Red Pepper Hummus

In a food processor
2 cups   cooked or canned Chick Peas (drained)
2 Tbsp   Lemon Juice
3 cloves Garlic minced
½ Small Red Onion
¼ cup   extra Virgin Olive Oil
1 tsp   Salt
1 ½ tsp   Ground Cumin

Blend together till smooth

Warm Tomato-Olive-Tapenade

3 tsp extra-virgin olive oil, divided
¼ tsp freshly ground pepper
1 tsp minced shallot
1 cup halved cherry tomatoes
¼ cup chopped cured olives
1 Tbsp capers, rinsed and chopped
1 ½ tsp chopped fresh oregano
1 tsp balsamic vinegar

Heat the remaining 1 tsp oil in a small skillet over medium heat. Add shallots and cook, stirring until beginning to soften, about 20 seconds. Add tomatoes and cook, stirring until softened, about 1 ½ minutes. Add olives and capers; cook, stirring for 30 seconds more. Stir in oregano and vinegar; remove from heat.

Artisans Salsa

2 cans of diced tomato 15 oz (drained)
¼ - ½ bunch cilantro
½   red onion diced
 1 - 2 seeds removed jalapenos
1 lime juiced
1 tsp salt
½ tsp pepper

Put all ingredients EXCEPT Tomatoes in food processor and pulse 2 – 3 times. Add tomatoes and process till desired texture

Guacamole

3 avocados, seeded and peeled
1 lime, squeezed
1/2 tsp kosher salt
1/2 tsp cayenne
1/2 medium red onion, diced
2 Roma tomatoes, seeded and diced
1 Tbsp chopped cilantro
1 clove garlic, minced

Directions:
In a bowl place the scooped avocado and lime juice, toss
to coat. Using a fork add the salt, cayenne and mash.
Then, fold in the onions, tomatoes, cilantro, and garlic.
Let sit at room temperature for 1 hour and then serve.

White Bean Dip

1 can (15 ounces) white (cannellini) beans, rinsed and drained
4 garlic cloves, roasted
2 tablespoons olive oil
2 tablespoons lemon juice

Directions
In a blender or food processor, add the beans, roasted garlic,
olive oil and lemon juice. Blend until smooth. Serve on top of
thin slices of toasted French bread or pita triangles. This is also
excellent placed on top of red (sweet) bell peppers cut into
squares.

Raisin Cinnamon Clusters

1 cup prunes
1 cup raisins
¼ cup water
1 cup Old Fashion oatmeal
1 cup slivered almonds
½ cup honey
1 tsp cinnamon
Pinch of Kosher salt

Direstions: Puree' in food processor, first three ingredients.
In large mixing bowl mix remaining ingredients. Add raisin
mixture and stir well. Form into golf ball sized balls on flat
pan.. Refrigerate

Instant Hot Spiced "Spark"Tea

In a large mug put;
1 scoop or packet of * Spark Mandarin Orange
½ teas. Instant tea
1/8 teas. Ground Cinnamon
1/8 teas. Ground Cloves.

Fill mug with hot water and stir

*Spark is the mental focus energy drink made by Advocare
        2 – 3 Tbsp of Tang instant orange juice may be
        substituted.

Salads

And

Dressings

Fresh Salsa Chicken Salad   Serves 4-6

Salsa:
28 oz can of diced Tomatoes (drained) or 3-4 roma tomatoes
½ diced onion (red or white)
½ to 1 seeded jalapeño pepper
juice from 1 lime
2-3 TB chopped cilantro.
Optional: ½ cup diced pineapple
              1 whole avocado diced

Combine salsa in a mixing bowl, set aside to let flavors combine.

2 boneless chicken breasts (8 oz ea)

Lettuce / salad mix/ fresh baby spinach

Pre heat on Medium burner a non-stick frying pan sprayed with E.V.O.O. (extra virgin olive oil)
Season chicken breast with salt, pepper and ground cumin.
Place meat in fry pan and cook till meat is well browned. Filp meat over and cook till done.

Put 1 large hand full of fresh baby spinach on a dinner plate. You may add some romaine, boston or spring mix lettuce if you like.
Cut meat into strips for easy serving and place on bed of greens.
Spoon Salsa mix over meat and enjoy.

Tropical Salsa on Salmon Salad   Serves 4-6

Salsa:
28 oz can of diced Tomatoes (drained) or 3-4 roma tomatoes
½ diced onion (red or white)
½ to 1 seeded jalapeño pepper
juice from 1 lime
2-3 TB chopped cilantro.
½ cup diced pineapple
1 whole avocado diced

Combine salsa in a mixing bowl, set aside to let flavors combine.

2 salmon fillets (8-10oz ea)
2 Tbsp sweet chili sauce

Pre heat on Medium burner a non-stick frying pan sprayed with E.V.O.O. (extra virgin olive oil)
Season salmon filets with salt & pepper .
Place fish in fry pan and cook 3 min. Flip fish over and glaze with sweet chili sauce, cook till done. Fish should just start to flake apart.

Put 1 large hand full of fresh baby spinach on a dinner plate. You may add some romaine, boston or spring mix lettuce if you like.
Cut meat into strips for easy serving and place on bed of greens.
Spoon Salsa mix over meat and enjoy.

Mediterranean Salad   (Fatoosh)

Dressing: for 1 serving
2 medium Garlic Cloves
1 – 1 ½ tsp salt
Crush in Garlic Press
Add: 1 TB + Lemon Juice

Mix well Add 2 TB olive oil

Drizzle over Salad of
Iceberg lettuce
Diced tomatoes
Chopped green onions
Chopped Flat leaf Parsley
Chopped Fresh Mint

Our Deepest Fear
By Marianne Williamson

Our deepest fear is not that we are inadequate.
Our deepest fear is that we are powerful beyond
measure.
It is our light, not our darkness that most frightens us.
Your playing small does not serve the world.

There is nothing enlightened about shrinking
So that other people won't feel insecure around you.
We were all meant to shine, as children do.
It's not just in some of us; it's in everyone.

And as we let our own light shine,
We unconsciously give other people permission to do
the same
As we are liberated from our own fear,
Our presence automatically liberates others

Chicken Red Bell Pepper Salad

Serves 3 – 4 people

Slice 2 – 3 raw chicken breasts
1 whole diced onion.
2 sweet Red bell peppers chopped   (or use roasted red peppers)
Salt & pepper to taste
One handful of grape tomatoes
1 bunch fresh spinach

Heat pan to medium heat spray with olive oil and sauté onion and sweet bell pepper until onion begins to caramelize, add chicken slices, season with salt & pepper
Add tomatoes and 2oz (1/4 cup) of water
Heat through until water evaporates, add one handful of spinach and cook till it wilts.

Dressing.
One whole sweet red bell pepper (or roasted red pepper)
 3oz balsamic vinaigrette ,
 1 oz evoo,
 blitz in food processor or blender.

Serve chicken mix over fresh spinach and liberally coat with dressing.

Artisans Chicken Salad

¼ cup   nonfat plain yogurt
¼ cup   Low Fat mayonnaise
1 tsp   season salt
¼ cup   finely diced red onion
1 tsp   celery seed
½ cup   seedless grapes, sliced in half
1 cup   diced pineapple drained
1 stalk   Celery diced fine
2 cup   skinless chicken breast, cooked and cut into ½ inch cubes
½ cup   coarsely chopped walnuts
1 medium apple, cored and diced

Mix well and serve on greens or in sandwich.

Southwest Salad

Serves 8

16 cup romaine
1 cup tomato, diced
2 cup black beans
2 cup frozen corn
1 cup black olives
1 cup red onion
4 cup chicken, diced
1 tsp cumin
1 Tbsp chili powder
1 tsp salt
¼ tsp pepper

16 oz Artisans Salsa   Page 22

Heat large pan to medium high heat, add oil, sauté onion and chicken, add black beans, corn and olives. Season with cumin and chili powder. Serve over salad and top with salsa

Artisans Curried Chicken Salad

¼ cup   nonfat plain yogurt
¼ cup   Low Fat mayonnaise
1 Tbsp curry powder
¼ cup   finely diced red onion
1 tsp   celery seed
½ cup   seedless grapes, sliced in half
1 stalk Celery diced fine
 2 cup   skinless chicken breast, cooked and cut into ½ inch cubes
1 medium apple, cored and diced
¼ tsp black pepper
½ tsp salt

Mix well and serve on greens or in sandwich.

"Do not wait; the time will never be 'just right'. Start where you stand, and work with whatever tools you may have at your command, and better tools will be found as you go along."

~Napoleon Hill~

Quinoa Salad

1 cup quinoa
1 cup frozen baby lima beans, thawed
2 Tbsp fresh lemon juice
1 Tbsp olive oil
1 cup red cabbage, shredded
1 cup carrots
¼ cup parsley
1 tsp lemon peel zest
½ tsp kosher salt
¼ cup feta cheese
¼ cup mint

Bring 2 cups water to a boil in a medium saucepan. Stir in quinoa. Reduce heat to medium-low; cover and simmer 10 minutes. Stir in lima beans; cover and simmer 5 minutes or until liquid is absorbed. Transfer mixture to a large bowl; l stand 5 minutes. Stir in remaining ingredients except feta cheese. Cover and chill at least 1 hour or up to 24 hours b serving. Top with feta

Bean Salad

Serves 4-6

1   15 oz can black beans (drained and rinsed)
1   15 oz. can pinto beans (drained and rinsed)
½ cup   banana chili peppers (drained)
½ cup   red onion, finely chopped
3 tbsp   extra virgin olive oil
2 tbsp   balsamic vinegar
2 tsp   kosher salt
1 tsp   ground cumin

Combine beans in a large bowl. Add chili peppers, red onion, oil, vinager, salt, cumin; mix well. Reserve 2-½ cups salad for Three bean Tacos. Chill up to 3 days. Refrigerate remaining 3 cups salad 30 minutes for flavors to blend. Serve over lettuce as a side dish or as a base for broiled and grilled fish.

Quick Mesclun Salad

Serves 4-6

1 Tbsp fresh lemon juice
1/2 tsp Dijon mustard
1/4 tsp sugar
2 Tbsp olive oil
5 ounces mesclun (8 cups)
1 pkg. cherry tomatoes
1 cucumber sliced

Whisk together lemon juice, mustard, sugar, and 1/2 teaspoon salt in a large bowl until salt and sugar are dissolved, then add oil in a slow stream, whisking until emulsified.
Add greens tomatoes and cucumbers to dressing and toss to coat. Serve immediately.

Apple Raisin Salad Dressing

Try serving over pork or chicken

Two large apples, peeled seeded and diced
1 tbsp brown sugar
1/3 cup golden raisins
¼ cup water
Simmer until apples are mushy
Mash apple raisin mix,

add 2 tbsp balsamic vin and 2tbsp honey mustard

Mix well.

Whisk in 1/3 cup extra virgin olive oil.

Season to taste.

Fall Salad   Serves 4

6 cups mesclun mix
1 ½ cups candied pecans (recipe on pg. 85)
1 cup dried cranberries
4 oz goat cheese crumbled
1 pkg cherry tomatoes
Maple Salad Dressing (recipe on pg. 36)

In a large bowl combine all ingredients except for
dressing. Toss to distribute evenly. Finish individual
salads with Maple Salad Dressing.

Maple Salad Dressing

4 TBSP Balsamic vin
2 tbsp Dijon mustard
Maple syrup to taste (around ¼ cup)
1/3 cup extra virgin olive oil

Directions: Combine first three ingredients and slowly whisk in olive oil.

Shiny Vinaigrette

8 Tbsp lemon juice
2 Tbsp Dijon mustard
1 tsp sugar
Salt and pepper, to taste
1/2 cup extra-virgin olive oil

Whisk together lemon juice, mustard, sugar salt and pepper in a large bowl until salt and sugar are dissolved, then add oil in a slow stream, whisking until emulsified.

Cucumber Dill Dressing

1 lbs. soft Tofu
4 oz Olive Oil
2 Tbsp Honey
1 cucumbers, peeled, seeded and quartered
1 Tbsp + 1 tsp Dill weed

Combine in blender and mix well till smooth.

Veggie Antipasto

For vinaigrette

3 Tbsp red-wine vinegar
1 small garlic clove, minced
1/2 tsp sugar
1/2 tsp salt
1/8 tsp black pepper
6 Tbsps extra-virgin olive oil

For salad

1 cup pickled onions pg 82
2 hearts of romaine (12 ounces total), torn into bite-size pieces
1 cup loosely packed fresh flat-leaf parsley leaves
1 (8-oz) jar roasted red peppers, rinsed, drained, and cut
lengthwise into 1/4-inch-thick strips
2 (6-oz) jars marinated artichoke hearts, drained
1 cup assorted brine-cured olives
1 cup drained bottled peperoncini (5 ounces)
1/2 lb cherry tomatoes, halved

Make vinaigrette:
Whisk together vinegar, garlic, sugar, salt and pepper in a
large bowl until salt and sugar are dissolved, then add oil
in a slow stream, whisking until emulsified.

Make salad:

Spread romaine on a large platter and scatter with parsley,
peppers, artichokes, olives, peperoncini, tomatoes, and onion.
Whisk vinaigrette again and drizzle over salad.

Beet Salad

1 small bunch beets, or enough canned beets (no salt added)
to make 3 cups, drained
1/4 cup red wine vinegar
1/4 cup chopped apple
1/4 cup chopped celery
3 tablespoons balsamic vinegar
1 tablespoon olive oil
8 cups fresh salad greens
Freshly ground pepper
3 tablespoons chopped walnuts
1/4 cup Gorgonzola cheese, crumbled

Steam raw beets in water in saucepan until tender. Slip off
skins. Rinse to cool. Slice in 1/2-inch rounds. In a medium bowl,
toss with red wine vinegar. Add apples and celery. Toss
together. In a large bowl, combine balsamic vinegar, olive oil.
Add salad greens and toss. Put greens onto individual salad
plates. Top with sliced beet mixture. Sprinkle with pepper,
walnuts and cheese.

SOUPS

Chili

(makes 12 – 15 servings)

1 cup dried black beans
1 cup dried great northern beans
1 cup dried red beans
(soak all beans overnight)

In a Large pot or dutch oven
Sautee following in 1 tbsp veg oil

1 onion diced
2 jalapeños
1 serrano chili
1 green pepper diced
1 red pepper diced
1 medium carrot chopped
2 stalks celery diced
2 cups chopped mushroom,
20 oz ground turkey.

Add 3 , 28oz cans of diced tomatoes with liquid.
Add 2 cups of low sodium chicken or veg stock.
Add 6 tbsp mild chili powder
Add all beans
Simmer for 2 hrs.   Season to taste.

Mushroom Barley Soup   Serves 6

½ cup pearl barley, raw
6 ½ cup vegetable stock
½ tsp salt
3 Tbsp tamari soy sauce
4 Tbsp sherry, dry
3 Tbsp butter (or olive oil)
2 cloves garlic, minced
1 cup onion, chopped
1 lb mushrooms, fresh sliced
1 tsp black pepper, fresh ground

Cook the barley in 1 ½ cup of the stock or water until
tender(cook it right in the soup kettle). Add remaining stock or
water, tamari and sherry. Saute onions and garlic in butter.
When the soften, add mushrooms and ½ tsp salt. When all is
tender add to barley, being sure to include the liquid the
vegetables expressed while cooking. Give it a generous
grinding of black pepper and simmer 20 minutes, covered, over
the lowest possible heat. Taste to correct seasoning.

Roasted Root Vegetable Stew.   Serves: 6

2 large rutabaga
1-2 large or several small parsnips
1 large carrot
1 large sweet potato
1 small celeriac root
1 medium onion
1 can (14 oz) of chic peas, drained
1 Tbsp. olive oil
Salt & freshly ground black pepper
1 tsp. dried thyme
1 tsp. freshly finely chopped rosemary
4 C. vegetable broth (or chicken)

Scrub and trim ends and any bad spots off of all the root vegetables. You may wish to peel some or all of the root vegetables. Preheat your oven to 450 F. To prep the vegetables for roasting, cut everything, including the onion, into 1 inch cubes. Place on a foil-lined cookie sheet or in a roasting pan. Add the chic peas to the chopped vegetables. Drizzle with oil and toss with your hands so everything is evenly coated. Rinse your hands and season the vegetables with a generous pinch each of salt and pepper and the teaspoon of herbs. Toss again with your hands and spread into a single layer.
Roast vegetables in the oven for 30-40 minutes or until they are beginning to brown. Meanwhile, bring 4 cups of vegetable broth to a boil in a large saucepan. When vegetables are done roasting, carefully add to the hot broth. Let soup simmer on medium heat for 10 minutes. Using the back of your stirring spoon, press some of the vegetables up against the side of the saucepan until they are smashed to help thicken the soup. Taste and adjust seasoning as needed

White Root Vegetable Soup   Serves 4-6

2 large rutabaga
2 large parsnips
1 large turnip
1 medium onion (white)
1 Tbsp. olive oil
Salt & freshly ground white pepper
3 C. vegetable stock
1 tsp. fresh thyme (to finish)

Scrub, clean and peel vegetables. Dice veggies to around 2"
cubes and simmer in vegetable stock with onion until very soft.
In VERY small batches (or you will be burned), blitz mix until
smooth and creamy. Season with salt and pepper, add olive oil
and fresh thyme to finish.

Jamaican Rundown Soup.   Serves 4-5

1 Tbsp olive oil
1 red onions diced
1 large carrot diced
1 green or red bell pepper diced
1 can black beans drained
1 cup heart of palm
1 cup chicken stock
2 cans lite coconut milk
Salt & pepper to taste

Heat oil in pot, add diced carrots and sauté for 2 min, add
onions and continue to sauté 2 min add rest of vegetables and
sauté 4 minutes. Add chicken stock and coconut mild and
simmer for 30 minutes, reducing to thicken. Season to taste
with salt and pepper.

Tomato Basil Soup   Serves 4-6

1 yellow onion diced
1 small carrot diced
1 rib celery diced
1 Tbsp olive oil
1 15oz can diced tomatoes
1 15oz can tomato sauce
1 cup chicken stock
1 tsp minced garlic
3 Tbsp fresh chopped basil
1 tsp oregano
Salt and Pepper to taste

Heat oil in pot, add onion, carrot and celery, cook until softened. Add tomatoes, sauce, stock and garlic and heat through. Add fresh basil and oregano and season with salt and pepper. Adjust seasoning according to taste.

Lentil Soup

Serves: 4

1 tsp vegetable oil
1 onion, diced
1 carrot sliced
4 cups vegetable stock
1 cup dry lentils (any color)
1/4 tsp black pepper
1/4 tsp dried thyme
2 bay leaves
dash salt
1 Tbsp lemon juice

In a large pot, saute the onions and carrot in the vegetable oil for 3-5 minutes until onions become translucent.

Add the vegetable stock, lentils, pepper, thyme, bay leaves and salt.

Reduce heat to a simmer. Cover and cook until lentils are soft, about 45 minutes. Remove bay leaves and stir in lemon juice before serving.

Chicken Vegetable Soup   Serves: 8

1 Tbsp olive oil
4 boneless skinless chicken breasts rough diced
2 medium carrots, chopped
2 stalks celery, chopped
1 parsnip, chopped
1 leek, chopped
1 cup green beans, chopped
2 tablespoons parsley, chopped
1 clove garlic, crushed and minced
6 cups chicken stock
salt & pepper

Heat pot on medium high heat. Add oil, chicken and all
vegetables except green beans, sautee until fragrant beginning
to brown. Season lightly. Add garlic and chicken stock, simmer
30 minutes add green beans and parsley and cook for 4 min.
Serve

"People can become anything that they want to
become. Everyone has the ability - all that is needed
is the will, a plan, and the power to put that plan
into action."

~Thomas D. Willhite~

Three Bean Chili

Ingredients:

1 can tomatoes, diced (15 oz)
1 can green chili
2 ea. jalapenos
1 can black beans (drained and rinsed)
1 can pinto beans (drained and rinsed)
1 can great northern beans (drained and rinsed)
1 bnch cilantro
1 tbsp chili powder (finish with more to taste)
1 tsp oregano
1 large white onion
1 tbsp olive oil
2 ea. limes

Sautee onion in oil. Add all and heat through. Season to taste.

Black Bean Soup

Serves 6 to 8.

1 Tbsp extra-virgin olive oil
1 large onion, finely chopped
3 or 4 cloves garlic, finely chopped
4 1-pound cans black beans, drained and rinsed
Juice of 1lemon
1 tsp ground cumin
1/2 tsp dried oregano
2 Tbsp finely chopped parsley
Freshly-ground black pepper, to taste
4 cups vegetable stock

Heat the oil in a large soup pot. Saute the onions over moderate heat until translucent, 3 or 4 minutes. Add the garlic and saute until the onion is lightly golden, another 3 or 4 minutes.
Add the remaining ingredients, except the toppings, along with the stock, and bring to a simmer.
Mash some of the beans with a potato-masher, just enough to thicken the liquid base of the soup. Cover and simmer gently but steadily for 10 minutes.

Serve hot topped with one or two of the optional toppings.

Optional toppings:

Green onions, thinly sliced, soy yogurt, reduced-fat sour cream, or low-fat yogurt.

Wraps

And

Sandwiches

Hummus Veggie Wrap

1 (12 inch) tortillas
½ cup   hummus   (recipe page 16)
1/8 cup cucumber
1/8 cup diced tomato
1/8 cup bell pepper
1/8 cup shoestring carrots
3 slices   red onions
alfalfa sprouts
lettuce

Microwave tortillas for a few seconds to make it pliable.
Spread the hummus over the tortillas. Add assorted
vegetables, adding the lettuce last. Roll up and slice in half or
eat whole. Enjoy!

"It's the little things you do that can make a big
difference. What are you attempting to accomplish?
What little thing can you do today that will make you
more effective? You are probably only one step away
from greatness."

~Bob Proctor~

Ginger Chicken Lettuce Wraps

Serves 4-6

1 yellow onion minced
1 Tbsp minced ginger
1 Tbsp minced garlic
2 chicken breasts cut into 1 inch strips
1 cup sliced water chestnuts
1 cup snow peas
1 cup mushrooms (shitake or your favorite blend)
½ cup shredded carrot

Large leaves of romaine lettuce cleaned and dried for wrapping chicken mixture in

2-3 Tbsp soy sauce
2 Tbsp Oyster Sauce
1-2 Tbsp sugar, to taste

Heat saucepan and lightly spray with oil. Add chicken, onion ginger and garlic. Saute until aromatic. Add all vegetables and sauté another 2 minutes, Add soy sauce, oyster sauce and sugar and cook another 2 minutes, scoop onto romaine leaves and roll.

Five-Spice Turkey & Lettuce Wraps

½ cup water
½ cup instant brown rice
2 tsp sesame oil
1 lb 93% lean ground turkey
½ cup diced onion
1 tbsp minced fresh ginger
1 tsp fresh minced garlic
1 large red bell pepper, finely diced
1 8oz can water chestnuts, rinsed and chopped
½ cup reduced-sodium chicken broth
2 tbsp hoisin sauce
1-2 tsp five-spice powder
½ tsp salt
2 heads boston lettuce,(or romaine) leaves separated
½ cup chopped fresh herbs, such as cilantro, basil, mint and/or chives
1 large carrot, shredded

Bring water to a boil in a small saucepan. Add rice; reduce heat to low, cover and cook for 5 minutes. Remove from the heat.

Meanwhile, heat oil in a large nonstick pan over medium-high heat. Add turkey,onion, ginger and garlic; cook, crumbling with a wooden spoon, until the turkey is cooked through, about 6 minutes. Stir in the cooked rice, bell pepper, water chestnuts, broth, Hoisin sauce, five-spice powder and salt; cook until heated through, about 3 minutes.

To serve, divide lettuce leaves among plates, spoon some of the turkey mixture into each leaf, top with herbs and carrot and roll into wraps.

Veggie Sandwich

Ingredients:

2 slices of Multi Grain Bread
1 tbsp   hummus   (recipe page 16)
1 oz   roasted red pepper
4 oz   cucumber
2 oz   spinach
3 oz   tomato
2 oz   pickles

Make yummy sandwich.

"If not us, who? If not now, when?"

~Kennedy, John F.~

Mushroom Philly

2 tsp extra virgin olive oil
1 medium onion, sliced
4 large Portobello mushrooms, stems and gills removed, sliced
1 large red bell pepper, thinly sliced
2 Tbsp minced fresh oregano, or 2 teaspoons dried
½ tsp minced freshly ground pepper
1 Tbsp all-purpose flour
¼ cup vegetable broth, or reduced-sodium chicken broth
1 Tbsp reduced-sodium soy sauce
3 ounces thinly sliced reduced-fat provolone cheese
4 whole-wheat buns, split and toasted

Heat oil in a large nonstick skillet over a medium heat. Add the onion and cook, stirring often until soft and beginning to brown, about 2 to 3 minutes. Add mushrooms, bell pepper, oregano and pepper and cook, stirring often until the vegetables are wilted and soft, about 7 minutes.

Reduce heat to low; sprinkle the vegetables with flour and stir to coat. Stir in broth and soy sauce; bring to a simmer. Remove from the heat, lay cheese slices on top of the vegetables, cover and let stand until melted, 1 to 2 minutes. Divide the mixture into 4 portions with a spatula, leaving the melted cheese layer on top. Scoop a portion onto each toasted bun and serve immediately.

Entrees

Pan Seared Tilapia

Heat sauté pan to medium high heat. Season tilapia with blackened seasoning, old bay seasoning, lemon pepper seasoning, salt and pepper or any other blend you prefer. Spray pan with non stick spray. Place fish in fry pan and cook till meat is well browned. Filp over and cook till done. Fish should just start to flake apart

Serve with steamed veggies and a sweet potato or brown rice.

Fish in Paper (or tinfoil)

Cous Cous
Cod, Tilapia, Whiting, Flounder,
2oz Orange Juice
1-2 oz white wine (optional) or water
Sliced veggies, onions, peppers, squash, broccoli, asparagus, etc
Salt and pepper to taste.

Place 3 oz dry cous cous on tinfoil sheet. Place filet on top and cover fish with veggies of choices, season according to taste and add orange juice and wine. Seal into a pouch and bake for an average of 10 min for a thawed fillet at 450 degrees. Fish and veggies will steam in bag, while liquid will reconstitute cous cous. Cooking time depends on fillet size. Bag will expand when done. Feel free to use seasonings that you normally would use with fish. Orange juice is used in recipe by lemons, limes or any other choice is just fine. Try a slice of Lemon in the pouch to finish with a wonderful citrus flavor.

Cod with Tomato Relish   Serves 4

2 tomatoes, diced, or one small can diced tomatoes drained
2 Tbsp fresh basil, chopped
1 tsp fresh oregano, chopped
1 Tbsp minced garlic
2 tsp extra-virgin olive oil
4 Cod, flounder or Perch, each 4 ounces

Preheat the oven to 350 F. Lightly coat a 9-by-13-inch baking pan with cooking spray.

In a small bowl, combine the tomato, basil, oregano and garlic. Add the olive oil and mix well.

Arrange the cod fillets in the baking pan, lightly season with salt. Spoon the tomato mixture over the fish. Place in the oven and bake until the fish is opaque throughout when tested with the tip of a knife, about 10 to 15 minutes.

Baked Salmon with Pineapple   Serves 2

1/2 cup pineapple juice
2 garlic cloves, minced
1 tsp low-sodium soy sauce
1/4 tsp ground ginger
2 salmon fillets, each 4 ounces
1/4 tsp sesame oil
Freshly ground black pepper, to taste
1 cup diced fresh fruit, such as pineapple, mango and papaya

In a bowl, add the pineapple juice, garlic, soy sauce and ginger.
Stir to mix evenly.

Put salmon fillets in a zip lock bag and add marinade from
bowl, refrigerate 1-2 hours.

Preheat the oven to 375 F. Lightly coat 2 squares of aluminum
foil with cooking spray. Place the marinated salmon fillets on
the aluminum foil. Drizzle each with 1/8 teaspoon sesame oil.
Sprinkle with pepper and top each with 1/2 cup diced fruit.

Wrap the foil around the salmon, folding the edges down to
seal. Bake until the fish is opaque throughout when tested with
the tip of a knife, about 10 minutes on each side.

Broiled Fish w/ Roasted Tomato Relish   Serves 4

3 cups cherry tomatoes, halved
1 teaspoon olive oil
1/4 cup chopped red onion
1/4 cup balsamic vinegar
½ teaspoon light molasses
1 tablespoon grated lemon zest
1 tablespoon chopped fresh flat-leaf (Italian) parsley
1/2 teaspoon salt
1/4 teaspoon freshly ground black pepper
1 teaspoon chopped fresh thyme
4 fish fillets (pick your favorite), each 5 ounces

Preheat the broiler (grill). Position the rack 4 inches from the heat source.

Arrange the tomatoes cut side down on a baking sheet lined with aluminum foil or parchment (baking) paper. Broil until the skins wrinkle and begin to brown, about 5 minutes.

In a frying pan, heat the olive oil over medium-high heat. Add the onion and saute until soft and translucent, about 4 minutes. Add the vinegar and molasses and bring to boil. Reduce the heat to medium and simmer until slightly reduced, about 2 minutes. Add the broiled tomatoes, lemon zest, parsley, 1/4 teaspoon of the salt and the pepper. Stir to combine. Remove from the heat, set aside and keep warm.

Lightly coat a broiler pan with olive oil cooking spray. Sprinkle the thyme and the remaining 1/4 teaspoon salt over the fillets and place on the prepared pan. Broil (grill) until the fish is opaque throughout when tested with the tip of a knife, about 5 minutes. Serve topped with the warm tomato relish.

Three Sisters

Serves : 4

1 cup	frozen corn
1 cup	zucchini, diced
1 cup	great northern beans
1 tbsp	extra virgin olive oil
1 tsp	thyme
1 tsp	basil
1 tsp	salt
¼ tsp	pepper
1 cup	tomato diced

Heat saucepan to medium heat. Add oil, then add corn, zucchini and beans. Heat through. Then add seasonings and dice tomatoes and cook until just heated through. Will keep several days in the refrigerator, re heat in microwave.

Can be served over cooked brown rice.

Stuffed Green Bell Peppers

Makes 4 – 6 servings

1 lb. lean ground beef or ground turkey
1 cup brown rice
1 15 oz can tomato sauce
½ small onion diced
Salt & pepper to taste

4-5 fresh Green Bell Peppers

In large mixing bowl combine first 5 ingredients and mix well.
Set aside.
Cut of tops and seed peppers. Rinse out to remove all seeds.
Drain well. Fill peppers with mixture and place in oven safe pan,
cook for 45 minutes in 400 degree oven.

In a hurry?

Place peppers upright in a large microwave safe baking dish. Fill
peppers with meat and rice mixture. Cover with wax paper or
loose plastic wrap. Microwave on high for 15 to 20 minutes.

Ratatoiulle
Serves 4-6

2 Tbsp olive oil
1 Tbsp garlic minced
1 small onion minced
1 tsp salt
4 grinds black pepper
1 diced red pepper
1 diced yellow pepper
1 diced orange pepper
2 sprig thyme stemmed and chopped
2 15oz cans diced tomatoes drained
2 Tbsp balsamic vinegar

Sautee first three ingredients then add diced peppers and cook 2 min and add tomatoes and thyme, heat through, add balsamic vinegar
Set topping aside

Slice the following fresh vegetables into uniform thick chips consistency and uniform size.

4 roma tomatoes
2 medium zucchini
2 medium yellow squash
1 eggplant
Lightly spray 9 by 13 pan with olive oil and layer sliced veggies until full.

Top veggies with pepper mix and bake covered at 350 for 2 hours, then finish uncovered at 400 for 15 min.

Lemon Caper Chicken
Over Brown Rice

Makes 6-8 servings

6   Boneless chicken breasts sliced
1 large onion diced
3 cups chopped fresh mushrooms
1   3.5 oz jar of Capers (drained)
 zest & juice from 2 lemons
1 cup chicken stock
Salt & pepper to taste

Spray a large skillet with E.V.O.O. and pre heat on medium heat.
Sautee onion lightly.
Add sliced chicken breasts and mushrooms.
Sautee till mushrooms are tender.
Add salt & pepper to taste, chicken stock, capers, lemon juice and zest
Bring to boil then reduce heat to low and simmer till chicken is done. The sauce should thicken to nappe consistency.

Serve over brown rice

In large sauce pan cook 1 ½ cups of brown rice according to direction for cooking rice

Mujadara
(Rice, Lentil, and Caramelized Onion Pilaf)

1 ½ cups basmati or long-grain brown rice
½ tsp salt, divided
1 Tbsp olive oil
1 large onion, thinly sliced (2 cups)
1 15 oz. can brown lentils, rinsed and drained, or 1 ½ cups cooked brown lentils
½ cup chopped fresh parsley
1 Tbsp chopped fresh thyme
2 tsp grated lemon zest
1 tsp ground cumin

Bring rice, 2 ¼ cups water, and ¼ tsp salt to a boil in a large saucepan. Cover, reduce heat to medium-low, and simmer 30 minutes, or until rice is tender, and all liquid is absorbed. Remove from heat, and let stand 5 minutes.

Meanwhile, heat oil in skillet over medium heat. Add onion and remaining ¼ tsp salt. Reduce heat to medium-low, and cook 30 minutes, or until onion is soft and browned, stirring occasionally.

Transfer rice to a large bowl, and fluff with fork. Stir in onion, lentils, parsley, thyme, lemon zest, and cumin. Season with salt and pepper, if desired.

Sweet Potato, Corn and Black Bean Fry Up.

Serves 5-7

2 tsp canola oil
2 medium onions, chopped
1 medium sweet potato, peeled and cut into ½ inch dice
2 large cloves garlic, minced
1 jalapeno pepper, seeded and minced
4 tsp ground cumin
½ tsp salt
¾ cup water
¾ cup frozen corn kernels
1 15oz can black beans, rinsed
2 Tbsp chopped fresh cilantro
Freshly ground pepper, to taste
1 lime, cut into wedges

Heat a large pan to medium-high heat. Add oil, and then add
onions and saute' until browned in spots, 3 to 5 minutes.
Add sweet potato and cook, stirring until it starts to brown in
spots, 5 to 7 minutes. Stir in garlic, jalapeno, cumin and salt;
saute' until fragrant, about 30 seconds. Add water and cook,
scraping up any browned bits, until liquid is absorbed, 3 to 5
minutes. Stir in corn and black beans and cook until heated
through. Stir in cilantro and season with salt and pepper.
Serve with lime wedges.

- **Grilled Cocoa Chicken**

4 Chicken breasts, boneless, skinless
Salt and pepper
2 oz cocoa powder
Spritzer olive oil

Heat grill, season chicken with salt and pepper, then dust all chicken liberally with cocoa powder. Spritz coated chicken with olive oil and grill until cooked through.

Blue Pear Pizza

1 tsp olive oil
1 medium yellow onion
1 cup spinach
1 pear
¼ cup walnuts
¼ cup blue cheese
Olive oil
2 whole wheat pitas (7inch)
Salt and Pepper

Heat pan on medium low heat, add oil and sliced yellow onion. Caramalize onion and set aside. Core and thinly slice pears, set aside. Preheat oven to 400 degrees. Brush pitas with light coating of olive oil, divide spinach between two pitas in even layer. Distribute onions on both pizzas. Cover surface of each pizza with pear slices. Top each pizza with remaining walnuts and blue cheese. Finish with dash of salt and two grinds of pepper. Bake on pizza stone for 10-15 min.

Veggie Bake

3 Sweet Potato
1 bag baby carrots
1 parsnip
1 rutabaga
2 large onions
2 packs whole button mushrooms
1 large yellow squash
1 large zucchini
Olive oil,
 Rosemary(fresh is best but dried is okay)
 Salt, pepper

Peel and cut potato into pieces roughly 1 inch by 2 inches
Combine in bowl with baby carrots spritz with olive oil and
season with rosemary and salt and pepper, put on
parchment paper in over at 400 degrees for 30 min, cut rest
of veg to similar size spritz and coat and add to tray after first
30 min. Cook for about 30 minutes or until veg is done to
taste. You will eat this like candy!!

Pork Tenderloin with Apples   Serves 4

1 Tbsp olive oil
1 pound pork tenderloin, trimmed of all visible fat
Freshly ground black pepper, to taste
1 cup chopped onion
1/2 cup chopped apple
1 1/2 Tbsp fresh rosemary, chopped
1 cup low-sodium chicken broth
1 1/2 Tbsp balsamic vinegar

Preheat the oven to 450 F. Lightly coat a baking pan with cooking spray.

In a large skillet, heat the olive oil over high heat. Add the pork and sprinkle with black pepper. Cook until the tenderloin is browned on all sides, about 3 minutes. Remove from heat and place in the prepared baking pan. Roast the pork for about 15 minutes, or until a food thermometer indicates 160 F (medium).

Meanwhile, add the onion, apple and rosemary to the skillet. Saute over medium heat until the onions and apples are soft, about 3 to 5 minutes. Stir in the broth and vinegar. Increase the heat and boil until the sauce has reduced, about 5 minutes.

To serve, place the pork on a large platter. Pour the onion-apple mixture over the top and serve immediately.

Sauteed Chicken with Kale and Mushrooms on a white bean puree. Serves 6

4 Boneless skinless chicken breasts sliced
1 bunch Kale, cleaned stemmed and chopped
1 Large yellow onion sliced
3 cups assorted mushrooms
1 Tbsp minced garlic
1 Tbsp extra virgin olive oil
Salt and Pepper to taste
White Bean puree Pg 82

Heat Pan to medium high heat and add oil, sauté kale and onion for three minutes, stirring often, add chicken, mushrooms, garlic and cook for another 7 minutes, until chicken is well browned. Season with Salt and Pepper.

Serve over white bean puree.

Pork Tenderloin with Sauerkraut Serves 6 - 8

Pork tenderloin 1-2 lbs
1 yellow onion sliced
1 jar sauerkraut
3 sweet potatoes peeled and rough diced
Salt and Pepper to taste

Season tenderloin with salt and pepper, place in crock pot, add all other ingredients and slow cook for 6 to 8 hours.

Baked Orange Chicken with Broccoli   Serves 6

6 skinless, boneless chicken breasts 6-8 oz ea
2 garlic cloves, minced
1 1/2 teaspoons extra-virgin olive oil
3 teaspoons fresh rosemary or 1 teaspoon dried rosemary, minced
1/8 teaspoon freshly ground black pepper
1/3 cup orange juice
Broccoli florets, six servings

Preheat the oven to 450 F. Lightly coat a baking pan with cooking spray. Rub each piece of chicken with garlic. Coat chicken with olive oil, then sprinkle with rosemary and pepper. Place the chicken pieces in the baking dish. Pour the orange juice over the chicken. Cover and bake for 25 minutes. Turn the chicken and return to the oven until browned, about 10 to 15 minutes longer. Baste the chicken with the orange juice from the pan as needed to prevent it from drying out. Microwave florets in glass bowl until they just begin to steam. Transfer the chicken to individual serving plates along with broccoli. Spoon orange juice from the pan over the top of the chicken and broccoli and serve immediately.

Butternut Squash Pasta   Serves 6

1 Tbsp olive oil
4 cup butternut squash, cubed and peeled
½ cup yellow onion, chopped
4 cloves garlic, minced
3 cup vegetable broth
2 cup whole wheat pasta (penne)
2 Tbsp sage, minced fresh
¼ cup cheese, parmesan freshly grated

Heat oil in a large saucepan over medium heat. Add squash and onion; saute 5 minutes. Add garlic; sauté acute; 1 minute. Add broth; cover and bring to a boil. Reduce heat to medium-low and simmer covered for 8 minutes. Stir in pasta; cover and simmer 12-15 minutes or until pasta is al dente and squash is tender. Transfer to shallow bowls; top with sage and cheese.

"Twenty years from now you will be more disappointed by the things that you didn't do than by the ones you did do. So throw off the bowlines. Sail away from the safe harbor. Catch the trade winds in your sails. Explore. Dream. Discover."

~Mark Twain~

Spaghetti Squash and Marinara   Serves 6

1 large spaghetti squash
1 tsp olive oil
1 small yellow onion, diced
2 cloves garlic, minced
1 can diced tomatoes (15 oz)
1 Tbsp Tomato paste
1 tsp dried oregano
1 tsp dried basic
Pinch thyme
Salt and pepper to taste
¼ cup cheese, parmesan freshly grated

Cut spaghetti squash in half and remove inner pulp and seeds. Place facedown in roasting pan with 1 cup of water and bake for 45 minutes at 400 degrees.

Heat oil in a large saucepan over medium heat. Add onion; saute 1 minute, add garlic, tomatoes and paste. Heat through, add herbs and season to taste.

Spaghetti squash should peel out of shell with fork into pasta – like threads, spoon marinara over squash and top with parmesean cheese.

.Three Bean Tacos   Serves: 8

2 ½ cups bean salad
8 oz artisans salsa
2 cup   cabbage blend, shredded
8 wheat tortillas
2 avocado; ripe, peeled, seeded, and diced
½ cup cilantro, chopped
1 oz low fat cheddar cheese
1 oz lite sour cream

Combine bean salad and salsa in a medium saucepan. Bring
to a simmer over a high heat. Reduce heat, stir well and
simmer 5 minutes or until heated through. Stir in cabbage
and heat through. Serve in warmed tortillas with avocado
and cilantro. Use cheese and sour cream sparingly.

"Look at a stone cutter hammering away at his
rock, perhaps a hundred times without as much as
a crack showing in it. Yet at the hundred-and-first
blow it will split in two, and I know it was not the
last blow that did it, but all that had gone before."

~ Jacob A. Riis

Red Beans and Rice   Serves 8

16 oz red beans, rinsed and drained
2 tsp Tabasco
1 Tbsp extra virgin olive oil
1 cup white onion, chopped
1 ea. large red bell pepper
1 cup carrot, thinly sliced
14 oz diced tomatoes
1 cup water
2 cups brown rice, cooked
1 tsp kosher salt
Tbsp thyme, chopped fresh
1 ea. large green bell pepper
1 Tbsp file powder

Combine beans and hot sauce in a medium bowl; set aside.
Heat oil in a large deep skillet over medium heat. Add onion;
saute' for 5 minutes. Add bell peppers and carrots; saute' 5
minutes. Add tomatoes and water; cover and simmer 6 to 8
minutes or until vegetables are tender. Stir in bean mixture
and file powder; simmer uncovered 5 minutes. Spoon rice
into four shallow bowls; top with bean mixture, salt and
thyme.

Vegetable Curry   Serves 4

2 -cans coconut milk, lite (6oz)
2 tbsp curry paste
1/3 cup red onion
1/3 cup carrot, diced
1/3 cup red pepper, diced
1/3 cup zucchini, diced
½ tsp salt
¼ tsp pepper
1 Tbsp curry powder
1 cup brown rice

Sautee onion and carrot in curry paste until onion is translucent and fragrant. Add coconut milk and simmer 2 min, add all others and heat through.

Cook brown rice according to directions.

"If you do not change direction, you may end up where you are heading."

~Lao Tzu~

Asian Noodle Salad with Peanut Sauce

1 cup peanut sauce natural
4 oz soy sauce
1 oz garlic
1 oz ginger
1 tbsp red pepper flakes
4 cup snow peas
4 cup brocoli
2 cup carrot, diced
1 cup red pepper, diced
30 oz pasta buckwheat
4 oz rice vinegar
40 grams cilantro

Cook noodles in water according to directions, steam veggies until crisp (microwave is okay), combine sauce in microwave and spoon over combined noodles and veggies

Dessert

Stuffed Apples

1/3 cup dried cherries, coarsely chopped
3 Tbsp chopped almonds
1 Tbsp firmly packed brown sugar
1/2 tsp ground cinnamon
1/8 tsp ground nutmeg
6 small Golden Delicious apples, about 1 3/4 pounds total weight
1/2 cup apple juice
1/4 cup water
2 Tbsp dark honey
Non stick vegetable oil spray

Preheat the oven to 350 F.
In a small bowl, toss together the cherries, almonds, brown sugar, cinnamon and nutmeg until all the ingredients are evenly distributed. Set aside.

The apples can be left unpeeled, if you like. Working from the stem end, core each apple, stopping 3/4 inch from the bottom.

Divide the cherry mixture evenly among the apples, pressing the mixture gently into each cavity. Arrange the apples upright in a heavy ovenproof frying pan or small baking dish just large enough to hold them. Pour the apple juice and water into the pan. Drizzle the honey evenly over the apples ,then spritz lightly with vegetable spray and cover the pan snugly with aluminum foil. Bake until the apples are tender when pierced with a knife, 50 to 60 minutes.

Zucchini Brownies

6 ounces bittersweet dark chocolate, chopped
1/4 cup vegetable oil
2 eggs
¾ cup granulated sugar
2 tsp vanilla extract
1 ½ cups all-purpose flour
3 scoops post workout recovery
1 1/2 tsp baking soda
1/4 tsp salt
1 1/2 cups shredded zucchini, (about 1 large zucchini)
1/2 cup chopped walnuts
Non-stick cooking spray

Preheat oven to 350 degrees F. Coat a 8×8-inch baking pan with cooking spray and gently coat surface with flour. Gently melt chocolate on low heat in microwave until soft.
Mix together the oil, eggs, sugar, vanilla and melted chocolate until well blended. Stir in the flour, post workout mix, baking soda, salt. Fold in the zucchini and nuts. Spread evenly into the prepared pan.
Bake for 25-30 minutes, until toothpick comes out clean when inserted in the center of the pan.

Fresh Dates with Honey and Greek Yogurt

Look for Dates in a ethnic foods store, serve with Greek Yogurt and a drizzle of honey for a sumptuous dessert.

Low fat yogurt (vanilla) with fresh berries

This refreshing dessert will satisfy your sweet tooth while leaving you feeling light and energized.

Chocolate Tofu Pudding

1 package soft silken Tofu
1 12 oz bag semi sweet chocolate chips

In microwave melt chocolate on medium power in microwave safe bowl, stirring frequently. Drain tofu and place it in a blender. Add chocolate to blender. Blend on high until mixed and a consistent chocolate color. Scrape into serving dishes.

Dark Chocolate- phase II

Chocolate cravings? Try a small piece of intense dark chocolate to curb your craving the higher cocoa percentage, the better.

Lite whip topping with frozen fruit.

I use this for strong cravings for ice cream. You get tons of flavor with a third of the calories.

Odds

and

Ends

Pickled Onions

1 medium red onion, thinly sliced (about 1 cup)
1/4 cup red wine vinegar or apple cider vinegar
1/2 teaspoon sugar
Kosher salt

Place onion slices in a medium bowl. Pour vinegar and 1/2 cup warm water over onion. Stir in sugar and season with salt; let stand until slightly pickled, about 30 minutes. Drain. DO AHEAD: Can be made 2 days ahead. Let cool slightly. Cover and refrigerate.

yield: Makes about 1 1/2 cups
This deeply flavored sauce is part barbecue sauce, part red-wine reduction.

White Bean Puree

1 can (15 ounces) white (cannellini) beans, rinsed and drained
2 garlic cloves
2 tablespoons olive oil
Water until smooth

In a blender or food processor, add the beans, garlic, and olive oil, blend. Add just enough water to allow mix to become smooth. Use as a base for chicken, fish or beef.

Ancho Chili Sauce

1 dried ancho chili, stemmed, seeded, torn*
2 tablespoons vegetable oil
1 ¼ cup chopped onion
1 tablespoon tomato paste
3 garlic cloves, minced
1/2 cup dry red wine
1/2 cup ketchup
1 tablespoon apple cider vinegar
1 tablespoon (packed) dark brown sugar
2 teaspoons Worcestershire sauce
1/4 teaspoon ground cumin

Place chile in medium bowl. Pour enough boiling water over to cover; let soak until soft, about 30 minutes. Drain, reserving soaking liquid.
Heat oil in heavy medium saucepan over medium heat. Add onion and sauté until soft, stirring often, about 4 minutes. Add tomato paste; stir 2 minutes. Add garlic and stir 30 seconds. Add wine and chili; simmer 2 minutes. Add 3 tablespoons reserved chile soaking liquid, ketchup, and all remaining ingredients. Simmer 3 minutes, stirring often. Season with salt and pepper. Remove from heat and cool slightly.
Puree sauce in blender, adding more reserved soaking liquid by tablespoonfuls if too thick. DO AHEAD: Can be made 3 days ahead. Cover and chill.
Use this sauce for chicken, veggies, it adds lots of flavor without lots of empty calories.

Radicchio, sweet and sour

2 tablespoons olive oil
1 ½ large onion, thinly sliced
2 tablespoons sugar
1/2 cup apple cider vinegar
2 large heads of radicchio (about 1 1/2 pounds), cored, each cut into 8 wedges
1/2 cup raisins
1 1/2 teaspoons salt
1/2 teaspoon ground black pepper
2 tablespoons toasted pine nuts

Heat oil in heavy large skillet over medium-high heat. Add onion and sugar. Sauté until onion is lightly browned, about 7 minutes. Add vinegar; stir to blend. Add radicchio, raisins, salt, and pepper. Cook until radicchio is just wilted, about 7 minutes. Transfer to serving dish; sprinkle with pine nuts.

This side dish is excellent with chicken or fish.

Candied Pecans

1 oz butter
2 oz brown sugar
1 ½ cups pecans

Heat pan on medium heat, add butter and brown sugar and stir to combine, when completely melted add pecans and cook stirring frequently for 5 min making sure to evenly coat pecans. Turn Pecons out onto parchment paper and allow to cool.

Index

Ancho Chili Sauce	Pg 83
Apple Raisin Salad Dressing.	Pg 35
Artisans Chicken Salad	Pg 30
Artisans Curried Chicken Salad	Pg 32
Artisans Salsa	Pg 22
Asian Noodle Salad with Peanut Sauce	Pg 76
Baked Orange Chicken with Broccoli	Pg 70
Baked Salmon with Pineapple	Pg 58
Bean Salad	Pg 34
Beet Salad	Pg 38
Black Bean Soup	Pg 48
Blue Pear Pizza	Pg 73
Broiled Fish w/ Roasted Tomato Relish	Pg 59
Butternut Squash Pasta	Pg 71
Candied Pecans	Pg 85
Chicken Red Bell Pepper Salad	Pg 29
Chicken Vegetable Soup	Pg 46
Chili	Pg 40
Chocolate Tofu Pudding	Pg 80
Cod with Tomato Relish	Pg 57
Cucumber Dill Dressing	Pg 36
Dark Chocolate- phase II	Pg 80
Fall Salad	Pg 35
Fish in Paper (or tinfoil)	Pg 56
Five-Spice Turkey & Lettuce Wraps	Pg 52
Fresh Dates with Honey and Greek Yogurt	Pg 80
Fresh Salsa Chicken Salad	Pg 26
Ginger Chicken Lettuce Wraps	Pg 51
Grilled Cocoa Chicken	Pg 66
Guacamole	Pg 23
Hummus Veggie Wrap	Pg 50
Instant Hot Spiced "Spark"Tea	Pg 24
Jamaican Rundown Soup.	Pg 43
Lemon Caper Chicken	Pg 63
Lentil Soup	Pg 45

Lite whip topping with frozen fruit.	Pg 80
Low fat yogurt (vanilla) with fresh berries	Pg 80
Maple Salad Dressing.	Pg 36
Mediterranean Salad (Fatoosh)	Pg 28
Mujadara (Rice, Lentil, and Caramelized Onion)	Pg 64
Mushroom Barley Soup	Pg 41
Mushroom Philly	Pg 54
Pan Seared Tilapia	Pg 56
Pickled Onions	Pg 82
Pork Tenderloin with Apples	Pg 68
Pork Tenderloin with Sauerkraut	Pg 69
Quick Mesclun Salad	Pg 34
Quinoa Salad	Pg 33
Radicchio, sweet and sour	Pg 84
Raisin Cinnamon Clusters	Pg 24
Ratatoiulle	Pg 62
Red Beans and Rice	Pg 74
Roasted Red Pepper Hummus	Pg 21
Roasted Root Vegetable Stew.	Pg 42
Sauteed Chicken with Kale and Mushrooms	Pg 69
Shiny Vinaigrette	Pg 36
Southwest Salad	Pg 31
Spaghetti Squash and Marinara	Pg 72
Stuffed Apples	Pg 78
Stuffed Green Bell Peppers	Pg 61
Sweet Potato, Corn and Black Bean fry up	Pg 65
Three Bean Chili	Pg 47
Three Bean Tacos	Pg 73
Three Sisters	Pg 60
Tomato Basil Soup	Pg 44
Traditional Hummus	Pg 21
Tropical Salsa on Salmon Salad	Pg 27
Vegetable Curry	Pg 75
Veggie Antipasto	Pg 37
Veggie Bake	Pg 67
Veggie Sandwich	Pg 53
Warm Tomato-Olive-Tapenade	Pg 22

White Bean Dip   Pg 23
White Bean Puree   Pg 82
White Root Vegetable Soup   Pg 43
Zucchini Brownies   Pg 79

Final Notes from the Authors:

We hope that this book will help guide you to a healthier more vibrant life. There is much that was neglected in this work, there is much more to do. If you have a recipe or tip you would like to see included send an email to davidshipwright@gmail.com and we will include it in the 2nd edition of this work.

Contact Info:

James Shipley

Jimshipley70@gmail.com

advocare.com/11098653/

Pam Heintz

jp@artisanscafe.net

advocare.com/110916541/

Made in the USA
Lexington, KY
25 August 2012